The Path to A Lifestyle of Humility

Insights from the Bible

By Scott Alan Richards

The Path to A Lifestyle of Humility

Insights from the Bible

Table of Contents

Introduction / Preface

HUMILITY, OFTEN OVERLOOKED in a world that glorifies success and self-promotion, holds a profound significance in the teachings found in the Bible. In this book, we embark on a journey through the sacred scriptures to explore the essence of humility, its manifestations, and its transformative power in our lives.

In a world often defined by ambition, success, and the pursuit of personal glory, the concept of humility might seem out of place, even antiquated. Yet, within the pages of the Bible, humility emerges as a cornerstone of spiritual wisdom and ethical living. It is a virtue that transcends time and culture, offering profound insights into the nature of human existence and our relationship with God.

This book, "The Path to A Lifestyle of Humility," seeks to explore the rich tapestry of humility as presented in the sacred scriptures. Through careful study and reflection, we will journey together to uncover the essence of humility, its significance in the lives of individuals and communities, and its transformative power in shaping our character and destiny.

The Bible serves as our guide on this journey, providing a reliable and authoritative source for understanding the principles of humility as they relate to our spiritual and moral well-being. Drawing from its timeless wisdom, we will delve into the depths of humility, examining its various facets, from its foundational principles to its practical manifestations in everyday life.

In a world that often elevates pride and self-aggrandizement, the message of humility offers a counter-cultural perspective, reminding us of the beauty and strength found in selflessness and humility. Through the examples of biblical figures and the teachings of Jesus Christ, we will discover how humility can enrich our relationships, enhance our leadership, and bring us closer to Jesus Christ.

As we embark on this exploration, let us approach with open hearts and minds, ready to embrace the transformative power of humility in our own lives. May this journey inspire and enlighten us, guiding us towards a deeper understanding of ourselves, our purpose, and our connection to God.

May the insights gleaned from the pages of this book serve as a beacon of light, illuminating our path as we walk in humility and grace.

Blessings to all who read this book,

Scott Alan Richards

Chapter 1
Understanding Humility

BEFORE DELVING INTO the depths of humility, it's essential to grasp its true meaning. What does it mean to be humble according to the Bible? Let's uncover the foundational principles that underpin this virtue. Humility, often portrayed as a virtue of meekness and lowliness, holds a profound significance in the teachings found in the Bible. Yet, to truly understand humility, we must first dispel misconceptions and grasp its essence as presented in sacred scripture.

The Foundation of Humility

AT ITS CORE, HUMILITY is not merely a behavioral trait or a show of modesty; it is a fundamental orientation of the heart and mind. The Bible lays the foundation for humility in its depiction of God's character and the nature of human existence. In the book of Proverbs, we read, "The fear of the Lord is the instruction for wisdom, and before honor comes humility" (Proverbs 15:33, NASB). Here, humility is intertwined with wisdom and reverence for God, suggesting that true humility begins with acknowledging our dependence on God.

At the heart of humility lies a deep recognition of our relationship with God. It is grounded in the understanding that we are creatures fashioned by the hands of a loving Creator, dependent on His grace and mercy for every breath we take and every step we make. Humility begins with acknowledging our inherent limitations and our need for God's guidance and provision in our lives.

Scripture paints a vivid picture of the foundation of humility, reminding us of our place in the grand tapestry of creation. In Psalm 139, the psalmist declares,

"Search me, O God, and know my heart! Try me and know my thoughts! And see if there be any grievous way in me, and lead me in the way everlasting" (Psalm 139:23-24). This prayer reflects a posture of humility—a willingness to open ourselves up to God's scrutiny and guidance, trusting in His wisdom and goodness to lead us in the paths of righteousness.

The foundation of humility is also built upon a deep reverence for God and His Word. In Proverbs 3:5-6, we are admonished to "Trust in the Lord with all your heart, and do not lean on your own understanding. In all your ways acknowledge him, and he will direct your paths." Humility requires us to surrender our own desires and plans to God's will, trusting in His sovereignty and providence to guide us in the paths of righteousness.

Contrasting Humility and Pride

TO UNDERSTAND HUMILITY, it is instructive to contrast it with its antithesis: pride. Throughout the Bible, pride is depicted as a destructive force that leads to downfall and estrangement from God. The book of Proverbs warns, "Pride goes before destruction, and a haughty spirit before stumbling" (Proverbs 16:18, NASB). In contrast, humility is portrayed as a virtue that leads to exaltation and favor with God. The apostle James writes, "But He gives a greater grace. Therefore, it says, 'God is opposed to the proud, but gives grace to the humble'" (James 4:6, NASB).

Humility and pride stand as contrasting pillars that shape the landscape of our hearts and minds. While humility leads us to a posture of openness, grace, and dependence on God, pride blinds us to our true selves, fostering an attitude of self-sufficiency, arrogance, and independence.

Humility is marked by a deep awareness of our own limitations and a willingness to acknowledge our need for God's guidance and provision in our lives. It is characterized by a posture of surrender—a recognition that we are but dust before the Creator of the universe, utterly dependent on His grace and mercy for every breath we take. "Whoever exalts himself will be humbled, and whoever humbles himself will be exalted." - Matthew 23:12

In contrast, pride is characterized by an inflated sense of self-importance and a desire for recognition and approval from others. It blinds us to our own faults and weaknesses, leading us to believe that we are self-sufficient and in need of nothing beyond ourselves.

Humility as Self-Forgetfulness

ONE OF THE HALLMARKS of humility is self-forgetfulness, a willingness to shift the focus from oneself to others and to God. The apostle Paul captures this sentiment beautifully in his letter to the Philippians, urging believers to emulate the humility of Christ: "Do nothing from selfishness or empty conceit, but with humility of mind regard one another as more important than yourselves; do not merely look out for your own personal interests, but also for the interests of others" (Philippians 2:3-4, NASB). Here, humility is portrayed as a mindset that prioritizes the needs and well-being of others above one's own, mirroring the selflessness of Christ. As we embrace humility as self-forgetfulness, we are reminded of the words of John the Baptist, who declared of Jesus, "He must increase, but I must decrease" (John 3:30). In a world consumed by self-interest and self-promotion, may we follow the example of Christ, who humbled Himself for our sake, and who calls us to do likewise.

Humility as Teachability

ANOTHER ASPECT OF HUMILITY is teachability, a willingness to acknowledge our limitations and learn from others. The book of Proverbs extols the virtues of humility in seeking knowledge: "He who is prudent will find good, and he who is wise is humble" (Proverbs 11:2, NASB). Humility opens the door to growth and enlightenment, allowing us to receive instruction and correction with grace and humility. An attitude of openness and receptivity to learning from God, from others, and from the circumstances of life. It acknowledges that none of us have all the answers and that there is always room for growth, development, and transformation. Humility as teachability is grounded in a recognition of our own limitations and fallibility. It humbles us to seek wisdom and guidance from God's Word, recognizing it as the ultimate source of truth and wisdom. "All Scripture is breathed out by God and profitable for teaching, for reproof, for correction, and for training in righteousness, that the man of God may be complete, equipped for every good work." (2 Timothy 3:16-17)

Cultivating Humility

WHILE HUMILITY IS A gift from God, it is also a virtue that can be cultivated through intentional effort and spiritual discipline. The apostle Peter exhorts believers to "clothe yourselves with humility toward one another, for God is opposed to the proud, but gives grace to the humble" (1 Peter 5:5, NASB). Cultivating humility requires a willingness to surrender our pride and ego, allowing God to mold and shape us according to His will. Cultivating humility is a lifelong process—a deliberate choice to align our hearts and minds with the character of Christ. It requires intentionality, discipline, and a willingness to surrender our own desires and agendas to the will of God "He has told you, O man, what is good; and what does the Lord require of you but to do justice, and to love kindness, and to walk humbly with your God?" (Micah 6:8) Cultivating humility begins with a recognition of our own need for God's grace and mercy. It requires us to acknowledge our own limitations and weaknesses, recognizing that we are utterly dependent on God for every breath we take and every step we make.

Conclusion of Chapter 1

IN THIS OPENING CHAPTER, we have laid the groundwork for understanding humility as presented in the Bible. Humility is not merely a superficial display of modesty but a profound orientation of the heart and mind, rooted in reverence for God and self-forgetfulness. It stands in stark contrast to pride, offering a pathway to wisdom, favor with God, and genuine selflessness.

As we continue our exploration of humility in the subsequent chapters, let us keep these foundational principles in mind, seeking to cultivate humility in our own lives and to emulate the example set forth by Jesus Christ, who humbled Himself for the sake of others.

Chapter 2
Examples of Humility in the Bible

THE BIBLE IS REPLETE with examples of humble individuals who walked closely with God. From Abraham to Moses, from David to Jesus Christ Himself, let's examine these examples and glean insights into their humble character.

Throughout the pages of the Bible, we encounter numerous examples of humility embodied by both ordinary individuals and revered figures of faith. These accounts serve as powerful testimonies to the transformative power of humility and offer invaluable insights into its nature and significance. Let us explore some of these examples in depth.

Moses: The Humble Leader

ONE OF THE MOST PROMINENT examples of humility in the Bible is found in the life of Moses, the great leader of the Israelites. Despite his remarkable accomplishments and close relationship with God, Moses remained remarkably humble. In the book of Numbers, we read, "Now the man Moses was very humble, more than any man who was on the face of the earth" (Numbers 12:3, NASB). This declaration underscores Moses' exceptional humility, which was characterized by a profound sense of dependence on God and a willingness to serve others selflessly. Despite being raised in the royal household of Egypt, Moses willingly chose to identify with his oppressed Hebrew brethren rather than bask in the privileges of his position.

Moses' humility is perhaps most poignantly demonstrated in his encounter with God at the burning bush. When God called him to lead the Israelites out of bondage in Egypt, Moses initially hesitated, doubting his own abilities and questioning God's choice. "But Moses said to God, 'Who am I that I should go to Pharaoh and bring the children of Israel out of Egypt?' (Exodus 3:11) Moses' humility is evident throughout his interactions with the Israelites. Despite facing constant grumbling and rebellion from the people he led, Moses consistently interceded on their behalf, seeking God's mercy and guidance.

Mary: The Handmaid of the Lord

ANOTHER EXEMPLAR OF humility in the Bible is Mary, the mother of Jesus. In the Gospel of Luke, we read Mary's response to the angel Gabriel's announcement of her miraculous conception: "Behold, the bondslave of the Lord; may it be done to me according to your word" (Luke 1:38, NASB). Mary's humble submission to God's will stands as a model of trust and obedience, despite the challenges and uncertainties she would face as the mother of the Messiah.

Mary's humility is further exemplified in her Magnificat, a hymn of praise and thanksgiving to God for His faithfulness and mercy. In this beautiful prayer, Mary acknowledges her own lowly state and magnifies the greatness of God, declaring, "For He has had regard for the humble state of His bondslave; for behold, from this time on all generations will count me blessed" (Luke 1:48, NASB). Mary's humility, characterized by a deep reverence for God and a willingness to embrace His plan for her life, continues to inspire believers around the world.

Jesus: The Ultimate Model of Humility

OF COURSE, NO DISCUSSION of humility in the Bible would be complete without considering the example set forth by Jesus Christ Himself. In the Gospel of Matthew, Jesus declares, "Take My yoke upon you and learn from Me, for I am gentle and humble in heart, and you will find rest for your souls" (Matthew 11:29, NASB). Jesus' humility was not merely a superficial display of modesty but a profound expression of His divine nature and mission.

Jesus' humility is evident throughout His earthly ministry, from His birth in humble circumstances to His death on the cross. Despite being the Son of God, Jesus willingly took on the form of a servant, humbling Himself to the point of death, even death on a cross (Philippians 2:6-8). His life of selfless service and sacrificial love stands as the ultimate example of humility, inspiring believers to follow in His footsteps and to emulate His humble attitude.

The Apostle Paul: A Servant of Christ

FINALLY, WE CANNOT overlook the example of the apostle Paul, whose life was transformed by a profound encounter with the risen Christ. Despite his background as a Pharisee and persecutor of the early Christians, Paul humbly embraced his calling as an apostle and servant of Christ. In his letters, Paul repeatedly emphasizes the importance of humility, urging believers to "walk in a manner worthy of the calling with which you have been called, with all humility and gentleness, with patience, showing tolerance for one another in love" (Ephesians 4:1-2, NASB).

Paul's humility is perhaps most strikingly illustrated in his own words: "But by the grace of God I am what I am, and His grace toward me did not prove vain; but I labored even more than all of them, yet not I, but the grace of God with me" (1 Corinthians 15:10, NASB). Despite his significant contributions to the spread of the gospel and the establishment of the early church, Paul attributes all glory and honor to God, acknowledging his own dependence on divine grace.

Conclusion of Chapter 2

THE EXAMPLES OF HUMILITY found in the Bible provide us with invaluable insights into the nature of true humility and its transformative power in the lives of individuals and communities. From Moses to Mary, from Jesus to Paul, these examples remind us that humility is not a sign of weakness but a mark of true greatness in the eyes of God. As we reflect on their lives and legacies, may we be inspired to cultivate humility in our own hearts and to follow in the footsteps of those who have gone before us, walking humbly with our God.

Chapter 3
The Nature of True Humility

HUMILITY IS MORE THAN just a demeanor; it's a disposition of the heart. What are the defining characteristics of genuine humility, and how can we cultivate them in our own lives?

Humility is a virtue often misunderstood and undervalued in today's world. It is frequently associated with weakness or lack of ambition, yet the Bible presents humility as a cornerstone of spiritual wisdom and ethical living. In this chapter, we will delve into the nature of true humility, exploring its essence, its characteristics, and its transformative power in the lives of individuals and communities.

Recognition of God's Sovereignty

AT THE HEART OF TRUE humility lies a recognition of God's sovereignty and our own limitations as human beings. The book of Psalms declares, "The fear of the Lord is the beginning of wisdom" (Psalm 111:10, NASB). This fear is not a trembling dread but a reverent awe—a recognition of God's majesty, holiness, and authority over all creation. True humility begins with acknowledging our dependence on God, our Creator and Sustainer, and submitting ourselves to His will. "Yours, O Lord, is the greatness and the power and the glory and the victory and the majesty, for all that is in the heavens and in the earth is yours. Yours is the kingdom, O Lord, and you are exalted as head above all." (1 Chronicles 29:11 NASB)

When we recognize God's sovereignty, we are liberated from the burden of self-reliance and self-sufficiency. We acknowledge that we are finite beings, dependent on God for every breath we take and every beat of our hearts. "The earth is the Lord's, and everything in it, the world, and all who live in it." (Psalm 24:1 NASB)

Recognition of God's sovereignty also leads to a posture of trust and surrender. We entrust our lives into His hands, knowing that He is faithful to His promises and that His plans for us are for our welfare and not for evil, to give us a future and a hope. "Trust in the Lord with all your heart and lean not on your own understanding; in all your ways submit to him, and he will make your paths straight." (Proverbs 3:5-6 NASB)

Ultimately, recognition of God's sovereignty leads to a life characterized by humility, as we submit ourselves to His will and His ways. We trust in His wisdom and goodness, knowing that He is working all things together for our good and His glory. "But he gives more grace. Therefore, it says, 'God opposes the proud but gives grace to the humble." (James 4:6 NASB)

Embrace of Our True Identity

TRUE HUMILITY ALSO involves an embrace of our true identity as beloved children of God. In his letter to the Romans, the apostle Paul writes, "For through the grace given to me I say to everyone among you not to think more highly of himself than he ought to think; but to think so as to have sound judgment, as God has allotted to each a measure of faith" (Romans 12:3, NASB). Humility does not mean denying our worth or diminishing our gifts and talents; rather, it means recognizing that all we have and all we are is a gift from God, to be used for His glory and the good of others. "See what kind of love the Father has given to us, that we should be called children of God; and so we are." (1 John 3:1 NASB)

Embracing our true identity as followers of Christ frees us from the need to constantly prove ourselves or seek validation from others. We find our significance and security in the love of our Heavenly Father, rather than in the fleeting approval of human beings. "But you are a chosen race, a royal priesthood, a holy nation, a people for God's own possession, so that you may proclaim the excellencies of Him who has called you out of darkness into His marvelous light." (1 Peter 2:9 NASB)

Embracing our true identity also enables us to live authentically, without pretense or façade. We no longer feel the need to inflate our accomplishments or hide our weaknesses, for we know that our worth is found in Christ alone. "For we are His workmanship, created in Christ Jesus for good works, which God prepared beforehand so that we would walk in them." (Ephesians 2:10 NASB)

Ultimately, the embrace of our true identity leads to a life characterized by humility—a recognition of our dependence on God and our need for His grace and mercy. As we embrace who we are in Christ, we walk in the confidence of His love, secure in the knowledge that we are fearfully and wonderfully made in His image.

Gratitude and Contentment

TRUE HUMILITY IS MARKED by an attitude of gratitude and contentment, regardless of our circumstances. The apostle Paul writes, "I know how to get along with humble means, and I also know how-to live-in prosperity; in any and every circumstance I have learned the secret of being filled and going hungry, both of having abundance and suffering need" (Philippians 4:12, NASB). Humility enables us to find joy and satisfaction in God alone, rather than in the fleeting pleasures and possessions of this world.

Gratitude is the antidote to pride and entitlement, reminding us of God's goodness and faithfulness in every aspect of our lives. It shifts our focus from what we lack to what we have, fostering a spirit of thankfulness and appreciation for God's blessings. "Give thanks in all circumstances; for this is the will of God in Christ Jesus for you." (1 Thessalonians 5:18 NASB) Contentment, similarly, is a fruit of humility, arising from a deep trust in God's provision and sovereignty. It is the ability to find satisfaction and joy in God alone, regardless of our external circumstances or material possessions.

"But godliness actually is a means of great gain when accompanied by contentment." (1 Timothy 6:6 NASB)

Gratitude and contentment go hand in hand, shaping our perspective and outlook on life. When we cultivate a heart of gratitude, we find contentment in God's provision, trusting that He knows what is best for us and will always provide for our needs. In a world that constantly tells us we need more to be happy, gratitude and contentment serve as powerful counterweights, reminding us that true joy and fulfillment are found in God alone. As we cultivate these virtues in our lives, we grow in humility, recognizing that every good and perfect gift comes from above, from the Father of lights.

"Every good thing given, and every perfect gift is from above, coming down from the Father of lights, with whom there is no variation or shifting shadow." (James 1:17 NASB)

Service and Sacrifice

A DEFINING CHARACTERISTIC of true humility is a willingness to serve and sacrifice for the sake of others. Jesus Himself exemplified this when He washed the feet of His disciples, saying, "If I then, the Lord and the Teacher, washed your feet, you also ought to wash one another's feet. For I gave you an example that you also should do as I did to you" (John 13:14-15, NASB). Humility is not passive but active, manifesting itself in acts of kindness, compassion, and selflessness towards others.

Service and sacrifice are at the heart of Jesus' example of humility. He came not to be served but to serve, and His life was the ultimate sacrifice for the redemption of humanity. "For even the Son of Man did not come to be served, but to serve, and to give His life as a ransom for many." (Mark 10:45 NASB) As followers of Christ, we are called to emulate His example of humble service. This means putting the needs of others before our own, seeking to serve rather than to be served. Service and sacrifice require humility because they necessitate setting aside our own desires and preferences for the sake of others. It means being willing to go the extra mile, even when it's inconvenient or uncomfortable. "And whoever wants to be first among you shall be your slave; just as the Son of Man did not come to be served, but to serve, and to give His life as a ransom for many." (Matthew 20:27-28 NASB)

True humility is demonstrated not only in grand acts of sacrifice but also in the everyday opportunities to serve those around us. It's found in the willingness to lend a helping hand, offer a word of encouragement, or simply be present for someone in need. As we cultivate a spirit of service and sacrifice in our lives, we reflect the humility of Christ and bear witness to His love and grace. May we be willing vessels, ready to serve wherever and whenever God calls, knowing that in doing so, we participate in His kingdom work and bring glory to His name.

Freedom from Pride and Self-Exaltation

TRUE HUMILITY IS DIAMETRICALLY opposed to pride and self-exaltation. The book of Proverbs warns, "Pride goes before destruction, and a haughty spirit before stumbling" (Proverbs 16:18, NASB). Pride is the root of sin, leading us to exalt ourselves above God and others. It blinds us to our own faults and weaknesses, preventing us from recognizing our need for God's grace and mercy. Humility, on the other hand, liberates us from the grip of pride, enabling us to see ourselves as we truly are—fallible creatures in need of God's forgiveness and redemption. It allows us to acknowledge our weaknesses and shortcomings, trusting in God's strength to sustain us. "Therefore it says, 'God is opposed to the proud, but gives grace to the humble.'" (James 4:6 NASB)

Humility involves a renunciation of the ego and a willingness to put aside our own desires and ambitions for the greater good. It is only when we humble ourselves before God and others that we can experience true freedom and fulfillment. Freedom from pride and self-exaltation leads to a life marked by authenticity and transparency. We no longer feel the need to impress others or maintain a façade of perfection, for we know that our worth comes from God alone. "Let another praise you, and not your own mouth; a stranger, and not your own lips." (Proverbs 27:2 NASB)

Humility also frees us from the need to compete with others or compare ourselves to them. Instead of seeking to outdo one another, we are able to celebrate the unique gifts and talents that God has given each of us, recognizing that we are all members of the same body, united in Christ.

"For by the grace given to me I say to everyone among you not to think more highly of himself than he ought to think; but to think so as to have sound judgment, as God has allotted to each a measure of faith." (Romans 12:3 NASB)

Strength in Vulnerability

CONTRARY TO POPULAR belief, true humility is not a sign of weakness but of strength. The apostle Paul writes, "For when I am weak, then I am strong" (2 Corinthians 12:10, NASB). Humility involves a willingness to acknowledge our weaknesses and vulnerabilities, trusting in God's strength to sustain us. It is through our weakness that God's power is made perfect, enabling us to overcome obstacles and accomplish His purposes. Humility enables us to embrace vulnerability as a pathway to intimacy with God and others. It allows us to lower our defenses and be authentic about our struggles and shortcomings, knowing that God's love for us is unconditional and His grace is sufficient for all our needs. "Therefore, confess your sins to one another, and pray for one another so that you may be healed. The effective prayer of a righteous man can accomplish much." (James 5:16 NASB)

Strength in vulnerability also fosters empathy and compassion toward others. When we are willing to share our own vulnerabilities, we create space for others to do the same, building deeper connections and fostering a sense of community and belonging."Bear one another's burdens, and thereby fulfill the law of Christ." (Galatians 6:2 NASB) As we cultivate humility in our lives, may we embrace the strength that comes from vulnerability, trusting in God's power to sustain us and His grace to transform us. May we boast in our weaknesses, knowing that in them, God's strength is magnified and His kingdom is advanced.

Continual Growth and Transformation

FINALLY, TRUE HUMILITY is characterized by a spirit of continual growth and transformation. The apostle Peter writes, "But grow in the grace and knowledge of our Lord and Savior Jesus Christ" (2 Peter 3:18, NASB). Humility involves a willingness to learn from our experiences, to receive correction and guidance from others, and to allow God to mold and shape us into the image of Christ. It is a lifelong journey of becoming more like Him, day by day. Humility is not a destination but a lifelong journey—a process of continually growing and becoming more like Christ. It requires us to constantly examine our hearts and minds, seeking to align them with the character of God "And do not be conformed to this world, but be transformed by the renewing of your mind, so that you may prove what the will of God is, that which is good and acceptable and perfect." (Romans 12:2 NASB)

Continual growth and transformation require humility because they necessitate a willingness to admit our need for growth and change. It means being open to feedback and correction, allowing God to prune away the areas of our lives that hinder our spiritual growth. "But grow in the grace and knowledge of our Lord and Savior Jesus Christ. To Him be the glory, both now and to the day of eternity. Amen." (2 Peter 3:18 NASB)

Humility also enables us to embrace the process of growth and transformation with patience and perseverance. We recognize that change takes time and that God is faithful to complete the work He has begun in us. "For I am confident of this very thing, that He who began a good work in you will perfect it until the day of Christ Jesus." (Philippians 1:6 NASB) Continual growth and transformation lead to a deeper intimacy with God and a greater effectiveness in serving others. As we become more like Christ, we are better equipped to reflect His love and grace to those around us, making a tangible impact on the world for His kingdom.

Conclusion of Chapter 3

IN THIS CHAPTER, WE have explored the nature of true humility. True humility involves a recognition of God's sovereignty, an embrace of our true identity, gratitude and contentment, service and sacrifice, freedom from pride and self-exaltation, strength in vulnerability, and continual growth and transformation. It is not a sign of weakness but of strength—a mark of true greatness in the eyes of God. As we continue our journey of exploring humility in the subsequent chapters, may we strive to cultivate these qualities in our own lives, following the example set forth by Jesus Christ Himself.

Chapter 4
Humility in Action

True humility is not passive; it's dynamic and transformative. Explore how humility manifests in our actions, words, and attitudes, impacting not only ourselves but also those around us. Humility is not merely a passive state of being, it is a dynamic force that manifests itself in our actions, words, and attitudes towards others. In this chapter, we will explore humility in action, examining how it shapes our interactions, influences our decisions, and transforms our relationships.

Service to Others

AT THE HEART OF HUMILITY is a willingness to serve others selflessly, without seeking recognition or reward. Jesus Himself set the ultimate example of servant leadership when He washed the feet of His disciples, saying, "If I then, your Lord and Teacher, washed your feet, you also ought to wash one another's feet" (John 13:14). Humility compels us to look beyond ourselves and to consider the needs of others, finding joy and fulfillment in acts of kindness, compassion, and service. Humility in action involves putting the needs of others before our own, whether it's through acts of kindness, compassion, or self-sacrifice. It's about seeking to alleviate the suffering of those around us and showing them the love of Christ in tangible ways.

"In everything I showed you that by working hard in this manner you must help the weak and remember the words of the Lord Jesus, that He Himself said, 'It is more blessed to give than to receive.'" (Acts 20:35 NASB)

Service to others requires humility because it necessitates setting aside our own desires and preferences for the sake of meeting the needs of others. "Do nothing from selfishness or empty conceit, but with humility consider one another as more important than yourselves." (Philippians 2:3 NASB) Jesus demonstrated the ultimate act of service through His sacrificial death on the cross. As His followers, we are called to emulate His example by laying down our lives for others in service and love. "This is My commandment, that you love one another, just as I have loved you. Greater love has no one than this, that one lay down his life for his friends." (John 15:12-13 NASB)

Service to others not only meets practical needs but also bears witness to the love and compassion of Christ. It is a tangible expression of the gospel message, demonstrating God's love in action to a hurting and broken world. "Let us not love with word or with tongue, but in deed and truth." (1 John 3:18 NASB) As we cultivate humility in our lives, may we be ever mindful of the call to serve others with love and compassion, knowing that in doing so, we reflect the heart of our humble Savior and advance His kingdom on earth.

Listening and Empathy

TRUE HUMILITY INVOLVES a willingness to listen to others with an open heart and mind, seeking to understand their perspectives and experiences. The apostle James writes, "Everyone must be quick to hear, slow to speak, and slow to anger" (James 1:19). Humility enables us to set aside our own agenda and ego, allowing space for others to express themselves and feel heard. In doing so, we cultivate empathy and compassion, building deeper connections and fostering mutual respect. Listening with humility fosters deeper connections and mutual respect in our relationships, as it communicates value and affirmation to those we interact with. "The heart of the righteous ponders how to answer, but the mouth of the wicked pours out evil things."(Proverbs 15:28 NASB)

Empathy is the ability to understand and share the feelings of another. It involves entering into someone else's experience with compassion and sensitivity, acknowledging their emotions and validating their struggles. "Rejoice with those who rejoice, weep with those who weep." (Romans 12:15 (NASB) Showing empathy requires humility because it requires us to set aside our own concerns and be fully present to the needs and experiences of others. When we show empathy, we mirror the compassion of Christ, who entered into our humanity and experienced our pain, offering comfort and hope to those who are hurting.

Forgiveness and Reconciliation

HUMILITY IS ESSENTIAL for cultivating forgiveness and reconciliation in our relationships. The apostle Paul exhorts believers to "be kind to one another, tender-hearted, forgiving each other, just as God in Christ also has forgiven you" (Ephesians 4:32). Humility enables us to let go of resentment and bitterness, extending grace and mercy to those who have wronged us. It allows us to prioritize reconciliation over retaliation, seeking healing and restoration in our relationships.

Forgiveness requires humility because it means relinquishing our right to hold onto resentment and bitterness, choosing instead to extend grace and mercy to those who have wronged us. "But if you do not forgive others, then your Father will not forgive your transgressions." (Matthew 6:15 NASB) Forgiveness is not easy, but it is necessary for our own spiritual well-being and growth. When we forgive others, we free ourselves from the bondage of unforgiveness and experience the liberating power of God's grace. "Bearing with one another, and forgiving each other, whoever has a complaint against anyone; just as the Lord forgave you, so also should you." (Colossians 3:13 NASB)

Reconciliation is the restoration of broken relationships, achieved through humility, grace, and love. It involves seeking mutual understanding, healing wounds, and rebuilding trust. "So if you are presenting your offering at the altar, and there remember that your brother has something against you, leave your offering there before the altar and go; first be reconciled to your brother, and then come and present your offering." (Matthew 5:23-24 NASB) Reconciliation requires humility because it means taking the initiative to make amends and seek forgiveness, even when we believe we are not at fault.

Reconciliation is a powerful testimony to the transformative power of the gospel, demonstrating God's love and grace in action as we seek to restore relationships and bring healing to brokenness. "All this is from God, who reconciled us to Himself through Christ and gave us the ministry of reconciliation." (2 Corinthians 5:18 NASB)

Gratitude and Generosity

HUMILITY FOSTERS AN attitude of gratitude and generosity towards others. The apostle Paul writes, "In everything, I showed you that by working hard in this manner you must help the weak and remember the words of the Lord Jesus, that He Himself said, 'It is more blessed to give than to receive'" (Acts 20:35). Humility enables us to recognize our own blessings and privileges, prompting us to share our resources and blessings with those in need. It shifts our focus from accumulation to contribution, from self-interest to the common good.

Gratitude is a posture of humility that acknowledges God as the giver of all good gifts and recognizes our dependence on His provision. "Every good thing given and every perfect gift is from above, coming down from the Father of lights, with whom there is no variation or shifting shadow." (James 1:17 NASB) Cultivating gratitude requires humility because it requires us to shift our focus from what we lack to the abundance of blessings that God has bestowed upon us. "In everything give thanks; for this is God's will for you in Christ Jesus." (1 Thessalonians 5:18 NASB) Gratitude is not contingent upon our circumstances but is a choice we make to recognize and appreciate the goodness of God in every season of life. "I will give thanks to the Lord with all my heart; I will tell of all Your wonders." (Psalm 9:1 NASB)

Generosity flows from a heart of humility that recognizes that all we have belongs to God and is given to us to steward for His kingdom purposes. "Each one must do just as he has purposed in his heart, not grudgingly or under compulsion, for God loves a cheerful giver."(2 Corinthians 9:7 NASB) Generosity requires humility because it means relinquishing our attachment to material possessions and being willing to sacrificially give to others in need. "But store up for yourselves treasures in heaven, where neither moth nor rust destroys, and where thieves do not break in or steal; for where your treasure is, there your heart will be also." (Matthew 6:20-21 NASB) Generosity is not limited to material wealth but extends to our time, talents, and resources, as we seek to be channels of God's love and provision to those around us. "And do not neglect doing good and sharing, for with such sacrifices God is pleased." (Hebrews 13:16 NASB)

Gratitude and generosity are powerful expressions of humility that reflect a heart transformed by the love of Christ. As we cultivate gratitude for God's abundant blessings and demonstrate generosity towards others, may we bear witness to the transformative power of humility in action, bringing glory to God.

Humble Leadership

EFFECTIVE LEADERSHIP finds its foundation in humility. Jesus taught His disciples, "Whoever wishes to become great among you shall be your servant, and whoever wishes to be first among you shall be your slave" (Matthew 20:26-27). Humble leaders prioritize the well-being of those they lead above their own ambitions and agendas. They lead by example, modeling integrity, compassion, and selflessness in their actions and decisions. They inspire and empower others, fostering a culture of collaboration and mutual respect. "The way of a fool is right in his own eyes, but a wise man is he who listens to counsel." (Proverbs 12:15 (NASB)

Humble leadership is characterized by a servant-hearted attitude demonstrating humility through their words and actions. They do not seek power or recognition for themselves but rather seek to empower and uplift those under their care. Humble leaders inspire excellence and growth in their teams by setting high standards and expectations while providing support, encouragement, and guidance. Rather than seeking to glorify themselves, humble leaders recognize and celebrate the contributions of their team members, empowering them to reach their full potential. By fostering a culture of continuous learning and improvement, humble leaders cultivate an environment where individuals thrive and succeed.

Servant leadership is at the heart of humble leadership, as it seeks to emulate the example of Jesus Christ, who came not to be served but to serve. They humbly embrace their role as stewards of God's resources, using their influence to bring about positive change and transformation in the lives of those they serve.

Conflict is inevitable in any organization, but humble leaders approach conflict with grace, humility, and a commitment to reconciliation. Rather than escalating tensions or assigning blame, they seek to understand the root causes of conflict and to address them constructively. By fostering a culture of forgiveness, empathy, and resilience, humble leaders turn conflict into an opportunity for growth and unity.

Ultimately, humble leaders leave a lasting legacy that transcends their time in leadership. They are remembered not for their titles, accolades, or achievements but for the lives they touched, the relationships they built, and the positive impact they made on others. By humbly serving and investing in the growth and development of their teams, humble leaders leave behind a legacy of empowerment, inspiration, and transformation.

Acceptance of Imperfection

HUMILITY INVOLVES AN acceptance of our own imperfections and limitations. The apostle Paul writes, "For by the grace given to me I say to everyone among you not to think more highly of himself than he ought to think; but to think so as to have sound judgment, as God has allotted to each a measure of faith" (Romans 12:3). Humility enables us to acknowledge our mistakes and failures without shame or defensiveness. It frees us from the pressure to be perfect, allowing room for growth, learning, and grace.

Genuine Humility in Success

FINALLY, TRUE HUMILITY is evident not only in times of struggle but also in times of success. The apostle Peter writes, "Humble yourselves, therefore, under the mighty hand of God, so that He may exalt you at the proper time" (1 Peter 5:6). Humble individuals do not boast or seek glory for themselves but acknowledge that all good things come from God. They use their talents and achievements to bless others and advance God's kingdom, rather than to elevate themselves above others.

Conclusion of Chapter 4

IN THIS CHAPTER, WE have explored humility in action, examining how it shapes our interactions, influences our decisions, and transforms our relationships. From serving others selflessly to listening with empathy, from cultivating forgiveness to leading with humility, the practice of humility is multifaceted and far-reaching. As we strive to embody humility in our daily lives, may we be inspired by the example set forth by Jesus Christ Himself, who humbled Himself for the sake of others.

Chapter 5
The Rewards of Humility

Contrary to worldly wisdom, humility brings forth rich rewards. We will Discover the blessings and benefits that accompany a humble heart, as promised in the Bible. Humility, often regarded as a virtue of selflessness and modesty, offers rewards that extend far beyond its outward appearance. In this chapter, we will explore the profound rewards that come from embracing humility in our lives, drawing insights from the wisdom of sacred scriptures.

Favor with God

ONE OF THE MOST SIGNIFICANT rewards of humility is favor with God. Throughout the Bible, we see numerous examples of God's favor resting upon those who humble themselves before Him. The book of Psalms declares, "For though the Lord is exalted, yet He regards the lowly, but the haughty He knows from afar" (Psalm 138:6). When we humble ourselves before God, acknowledging His sovereignty and seeking His will above our own, we invite His presence and blessing into our lives.

Finding favor with God is a profound blessing that comes to those who walk in humility and obedience to His will. God's favor is not earned through our own efforts but is a gift bestowed upon those who humbly submit to His authority and seek His righteousness. "But He gives a greater grace. Therefore it says, 'God is opposed to the proud, but gives grace to the humble.'"(James 4:6 NASB) Finding favor with God results in His divine intervention and provision in our lives, as He works all things together His glory.

God's favor opens doors of opportunity in our endeavors. He guides our steps and leads us into paths of righteousness for His name's sake. As we walk in humility before Him, may we continually seek His favor, knowing that in His presence is fullness of joy and at His right hand are pleasures forevermore.

Wisdom and Guidance

HUMILITY OPENS THE door to wisdom and guidance from God. The book of Proverbs declares, "The fear of the Lord is the instruction for wisdom, and before honor comes humility" (Proverbs 15:33). When we humble ourselves before God, recognizing our own limitations and dependence on His wisdom, He promises to guide us in the paths of righteousness and to give us the discernment we need to navigate life's challenges. "But if any of you lacks wisdom, let him ask of God, who gives to all generously and without reproach, and it will be given to him." (James 1:5 NASB) God grants wisdom to those who humbly submit to His will, enabling them to make wise decisions and discern the path He has set before them. Humility opens our hearts to receive divine guidance, as we trust in God's sovereignty and providence to direct our steps. God promises to guide and instruct those who humbly seek His will.

Inner Peace and Contentment

HUMILITY BRINGS INNER peace and contentment, regardless of our external circumstances. The apostle Paul writes, "And the peace of God, which surpasses all comprehension, will guard your hearts and your minds in Christ Jesus" (Philippians 4:7). When we humble ourselves before God, surrendering our worries and anxieties to Him, He fills us with a peace that transcends understanding, enabling us to rest in His presence and trust in His provision.

Humility fosters inner peace by enabling us to surrender our worries, fears, and anxieties to God, trusting in His sovereignty and goodness. God's peace transcends understanding, calming our restless hearts and minds as we rest in His unfailing love and care. "Peace I leave with you; My peace I give to you; not as the world gives do I give to you. Do not let your heart be troubled, nor let it be fearful." (John 14:27 NASB) Humility breeds contentment by teaching us to find satisfaction in God alone, rather than in the fleeting pleasures of this world. "But godliness actually is a means of great gain when accompanied by contentment." (1 Timothy 6:6 NASB)

Exaltation in Due Time

IRONICALLY, ONE OF the rewards of humility is exaltation. Jesus Himself taught, "For everyone who exalts himself will be humbled, and he who humbles himself will be exalted" (Luke 14:11). When we humble ourselves before God and others, seeking to serve rather than to be served, He promises to lift us up in due time, honoring us before men and granting us a place of honor in His kingdom. "Humble yourselves in the presence of the Lord, and He will exalt you." (James 4:10 NASB) Exaltation by God is not dependent on human efforts or achievements but is a gracious gift bestowed upon those who trust in His unfailing love and faithfulness.

Humility often precedes promotion and recognition, as God honors those who serve Him faithfully and humbly in their respective roles and responsibilities. "The reward of humility and the fear of the Lord are riches, honor and life."(Proverbs 22:4 NASB) God sees the humble heart and rewards it openly, granting favor and blessing to those who walk in humility before Him. "He leads the humble in justice, and He teaches the humble His way." (Psalm 25:9 NASB)

Blessings in Relationships

HUMILITY FOSTERS DEEP and meaningful relationships with others. The apostle Paul writes, "Do nothing from selfishness or empty conceit, but with humility of mind regard one another as more important than yourselves" (Philippians 2:3). When we humble ourselves before others, putting their needs and interests above our own, we build trust and rapport, fostering a spirit of unity and cooperation in our relationships. "With all humility and gentleness, with patience, showing tolerance for one another in love, being diligent to preserve the unity of the Spirit in the bond of peace." (Ephesians 4:2-3 NASB)

Strength and Resilience

HUMILITY EMPOWERS US to face life's challenges with strength and resilience. The apostle Peter writes, "Humble yourselves, therefore, under the mighty hand of God, that He may exalt you at the proper time, casting all your anxiety on Him, because He cares for you" (1 Peter 5:6-7). When we humble ourselves before God, acknowledging our dependence on Him for strength and guidance, He promises to sustain us through every trial and adversity, enabling us to emerge stronger and more resilient than before.

"But He said to me, 'My grace is sufficient for you, for power is perfected in weakness.' Therefore, I will rather boast about my weaknesses, so that the power of Christ may dwell in me." (2 Corinthians 12:9 NASB) God promises to strengthen the humble and give them the courage and endurance to overcome obstacles and persevere in the face of adversity. "Yet those who wait for the Lord will gain new strength; they will mount up with wings like eagles, they will run and not get tired, they will walk and not become weary." (Isaiah 40:31 NASB)

Eternal Rewards

ULTIMATELY, THE REWARDS of humility extend beyond this life to the life to come. Jesus taught, "Blessed are the meek, for they shall inherit the earth" (Matthew 5:5). When we humble ourselves before God and live lives characterized by meekness and humility, we store up treasures in heaven, where moth and rust do not destroy, and where thieves do not break in and steal (Matthew 6:20). Humility yields eternal rewards that far surpass the temporal blessings of this world. Humility leads to the accumulation of heavenly treasures, as it prioritizes the eternal over the temporary and invests in the kingdom of God. God promises to reward the humble with everlasting riches and glory in His eternal kingdom, where they will enjoy fellowship with Him for all eternity.

Conclusion of Chapter 5

IN THIS CHAPTER, WE have explored the profound rewards that come from embracing humility in our lives. From favor with God to wisdom and guidance, from inner peace and contentment to exaltation in due time, the rewards of humility are manifold and far-reaching. As we humble ourselves before God and others, may we experience the rich blessings and abundant grace that flow from lives marked by humility and surrender.

Chapter 6
Overcoming Pride

PRIDE, HUMILITY'S ANTITHESIS, often poses a significant obstacle on our journey towards humility. Learn how to identify and overcome the pitfalls of pride that hinder our spiritual growth. Pride, often described as the root of all sin, poses a significant obstacle on our journey towards humility and spiritual growth. In this chapter, we will explore the insidious nature of pride, its detrimental effects on our lives, and practical strategies for overcoming it, drawing insights from the wisdom of sacred scriptures.

The Nature of Pride

PRIDE IS A PERVASIVE and insidious vice that manifests itself in various forms, from arrogance and self-righteousness to vanity and self-promotion. The book of Proverbs warns, "Pride goes before destruction, and a haughty spirit before stumbling" (Proverbs 16:18). Pride blinds us to our own faults and weaknesses, leading us to exalt ourselves above others and to reject the counsel and correction of God and others.

The Destructive Effects of Pride

PRIDE HAS DESTRUCTIVE effects on every aspect of our lives, from our relationship with God to our relationships with others and even to our own well-being. The apostle James writes, "But He gives a greater grace. Therefore it says, 'God is opposed to the proud, but gives grace to the humble'" (James 4:6). When we allow pride to reign in our hearts, we alienate ourselves from God's grace and mercy, hindering our spiritual growth and distancing ourselves from His presence.

Humility as the Antidote to Pride

THE ANTIDOTE TO PRIDE is humility—a recognition of our own limitations and dependence on God's grace. The apostle Peter exhorts believers to "humble yourselves, therefore, under the mighty hand of God, that He may exalt you at the proper time" (1 Peter 5:6). Humility involves a willingness to acknowledge our faults and weaknesses, to submit ourselves to God's will, and to receive His grace and mercy with gratitude and humility.

Cultivating Humility through Self-Reflection

ONE OF THE MOST EFFECTIVE ways to overcome pride is through self-reflection and examination of conscience. The psalmist writes, "Search me, O God, and know my heart; try me and know my anxious thoughts; and see if there be any hurtful way in me, and lead me in the everlasting way" (Psalm 139:23-24). When we humbly submit ourselves to God's scrutiny, asking Him to reveal any prideful attitudes or behaviors within us, He promises to lead us in the path of humility and righteousness.

Seeking Accountability and Feedback

ANOTHER IMPORTANT STRATEGY for overcoming pride is seeking accountability and feedback from others. The book of Proverbs declares, "Iron sharpens iron, so one man sharpens another" (Proverbs 27:17). When we invite trusted friends, mentors, and spiritual advisors into our lives to provide honest feedback and accountability, we open ourselves up to growth and transformation, allowing God to prune away the pride that hinders our spiritual progress.

Practicing Gratitude and Humility

GRATITUDE IS A POWERFUL antidote to pride, reminding us of our dependence on God and His abundant blessings in our lives. The apostle Paul writes, "In everything give thanks; for this is God's will for you in Christ Jesus" (1 Thessalonians 5:18). When we cultivate a spirit of gratitude and humility, acknowledging God as the source of all good things, we guard against the prideful attitude of entitlement and self-sufficiency.

Embracing a Servant's Heart

FINALLY, ONE OF THE most effective ways to overcome pride is by embracing a servant's heart—a willingness to serve others selflessly and sacrificially. Jesus Himself taught, "Whoever wishes to become great among you shall be your servant, and whoever wishes to be first among you shall be your slave" (Matthew 20:26-27). When we humble ourselves before God and others, seeking to serve rather than to be served, we emulate the example set forth by Jesus Himself, who humbled Himself for the sake of others.

Conclusion of Chapter 6

IN THIS CHAPTER, WE have explored the insidious nature of pride, its destructive effects on our lives, and practical strategies for overcoming it. From cultivating humility through self-reflection to seeking accountability and feedback from others, from practicing gratitude and humility to embracing a servant's heart, there are many ways in which we can overcome pride and cultivate a spirit of humility in our lives. As we humble ourselves before God and others, may we experience the rich blessings and abundant grace that come from lives marked by humility and surrender.

Chapter 7
Cultivating Humility in Daily Life

HUMILITY IS NOT A ONE-time achievement but a lifelong pursuit. We need to explore practical strategies and spiritual disciplines that foster humility in our everyday experiences.

Humility is not merely a theoretical concept or a lofty ideal; it is a practical virtue that can be cultivated and applied in our daily lives. In this chapter, we will explore practical ways to cultivate humility in our thoughts, words, and actions, drawing insights from the wisdom of sacred scriptures.

Practicing Gratitude

GRATITUDE IS A POWERFUL antidote to pride, reminding us of our dependence on God and His abundant blessings in our lives. Each day, take time to reflect on the blessings you have received, both big and small. Cultivate a spirit of gratitude by keeping a gratitude journal, regularly thanking God for His provision, and expressing appreciation to others for their kindness and support.

Embracing Vulnerability

HUMILITY INVOLVES AN acceptance of our own imperfections and vulnerabilities. Rather than trying to hide or deny our weaknesses, embrace them as opportunities for growth and learning. Share your struggles and failures with trusted friends or mentors, allowing them to offer support and encouragement. By embracing vulnerability, we open ourselves up to God's grace and transformation.

Seeking Feedback and Accountability

SEEKING FEEDBACK AND accountability from others is essential for cultivating humility. Invite trusted friends, mentors, or spiritual advisors into your life to provide honest feedback and accountability. Listen humbly to their insights and perspectives, even if they are difficult to hear. Use their feedback as an opportunity for self-reflection and growth, allowing God to prune away the pride that hinders your spiritual progress.

Serving Others Selflessly

ONE OF THE MOST EFFECTIVE ways to cultivate humility is by serving others selflessly. Discover your God-given gifts and use them in the practice of service in ministry, in the local church, mission trips Etc. Look for opportunities to serve those in need, both within your community and beyond. Volunteer at a local shelter, participate in a service project, or simply lend a helping hand to a neighbor in need. By putting the needs of others before your own, you emulate the example set forth by Jesus Himself, who came not to be served but to serve (Matthew 20:28). Acts of humble service enrich our lives in profound and meaningful ways. When we serve others selflessly, we experience a sense of fulfillment and purpose that cannot be found in self-serving pursuits. Service opens our hearts to the needs of others, fostering empathy, compassion, and connection. It reminds us of our common humanity regardless of our differences.

Living Out Our Faith

FOR CHRISTIANS, HUMBLE service is not just a moral imperative but a sacred duty. The apostle James writes, "Pure and undefiled religion in the sight of our God and Father is this: to visit orphans and widows in their distress, and to keep oneself unstained by the world" (James 1:27). Humble service is an expression of our love for God and our commitment to following in the footsteps of Jesus, who came not to be served but to serve. It is a tangible way of living out our faith and demonstrating God's love to others.

Practicing Active Listening

ACTIVE LISTENING IS an essential skill for cultivating humility in our interactions with others. Rather than focusing on formulating your response or waiting for your turn to speak, genuinely listen to what the other person is saying. Seek to understand their perspective and feelings without judgment or interruption. By practicing active listening, you demonstrate humility by valuing the thoughts and experiences of others.

Responding with Grace and Forgiveness

RESPONDING WITH GRACE and forgiveness is another hallmark of humility. When others wrong or offend you, resist the temptation to retaliate or hold onto resentment. Instead, choose to respond with grace and forgiveness, extending the same mercy that God has shown you. By forgiving others and letting go of grudges, you free yourself from the burden of bitterness and pride, opening your heart to God's healing and reconciliation.

Conclusion of Chapter 7

IN THIS CHAPTER, WE have explored practical ways to cultivate humility in our daily lives. From practicing gratitude and embracing vulnerability to seeking feedback and accountability, from serving others selflessly to practicing active listening and responding with grace and forgiveness, there are many ways in which we can cultivate humility in our thoughts, words, and actions. As we strive to embody humility in our daily lives, may we experience the rich blessings and abundant grace that come from lives marked by humility and surrender.

Chapter 8
Humility in Relationships

HEALTHY RELATIONSHIPS thrive in an environment of humility. Will now discover how humility fosters empathy, understanding, and reconciliation in our interactions with others.

Relationships are the intricate tapestry of human connection, woven from threads of understanding, empathy, and respect. In this chapter, we delve into the profound impact of humility on nurturing and sustaining healthy, meaningful relationships, exploring how it fosters empathy, resolves conflicts, and deepens intimacy.

The Essence of Humility in Relationships

AT THE HEART OF EVERY strong relationship lies humility—the willingness to set aside ego and pride in favor of understanding and empathy. Humility in relationships means acknowledging our imperfections, listening with an open heart, and valuing the perspectives and feelings of others. It forms the bedrock upon which trust, respect, and intimacy are built.

Fostering Empathy and Understanding

HUMILITY OPENS THE door to empathy, allowing us to truly understand and appreciate the experiences and emotions of our loved ones. When we approach relationships with humility, we are more attuned to the needs and feelings of others, creating space for deep, meaningful connections to flourish. By stepping into another's shoes with humility and compassion, we bridge the gap between us, fostering mutual understanding and empathy. Empathy is the ability to understand and share the feelings of another person, putting ourselves in their place and seeing the world through their eyes. "Be kind to one another, tender-hearted, forgiving each other, just as God in Christ also has forgiven you." (Ephesians 4:32 NASB)Jesus exemplified empathy in His earthly ministry, demonstrating compassion and understanding towards those He encountered, meeting them at their point of need.

"For we do not have a high priest who cannot sympathize with our weaknesses, but One who has been tempted in all things as we are, yet without sin." (Hebrews 4:15 NASB)

Resolving Conflicts with Grace

CONFLICT IS INEVITABLE in any relationship, but humility equips us with the tools to navigate disagreements with grace and compassion. Rather than seeking to prove ourselves right or assign blame, humility allows us to approach conflict with an open mind and a willingness to listen. By humbly acknowledging our own role in the conflict and showing empathy towards the other person's perspective, we pave the way for resolution and reconciliation.

Resolving conflicts with grace is a vital aspect of cultivating humility in our relationships. Resolving conflicts with grace involves extending forgiveness, compassion, and understanding to those with whom we have disagreements or conflicts. "Be kind to one another, tender-hearted, forgiving each other, just as God in Christ also has forgiven you." (Ephesians 4:32 NASB) Jesus Christ exemplified grace in His interactions with others, offering forgiveness and reconciliation even to those who wronged Him. "But I say to you, love your enemies and pray for those who persecute you." (Matthew 5:44 (NASB)

Humility is essential in conflict resolution, as it enables us to approach conflicts with a spirit of meekness, gentleness, and openness to reconciliation."Blessed are the peacemakers, for they shall be called sons of God."(Matthew 5:9 NASB)

Cultivating Intimacy and Vulnerability

TRUE INTIMACY REQUIRES vulnerability, and humility creates a safe space for both partners to be open and authentic with each other. When we approach relationships with humility, we are more willing to share our fears, insecurities, and deepest desires, knowing that we will be met with acceptance and understanding. By embracing vulnerability with humility, we deepen our connections and foster intimacy that is built on trust and mutual respect.

The Bible emphasizes the importance of deep, meaningful relationships built on trust, honesty, and vulnerability. "Therefore, confess your sins to one another, and pray for one another so that you may be healed. The effective prayer of a righteous man can accomplish much." (James 5:16 NASB) God calls us to cultivate intimacy and vulnerability by confessing our sins and struggles to one another, fostering an environment of trust, support, and accountability. "Two are better than one because they have a good return for their labor. For if either of them falls, the one will lift up his companion. But woe to the one who falls when there is not another to lift him up." (Ecclesiastes 4:9-10 NASB) God designed us for community and fellowship, where we can share our joys and sorrows, strengths and weaknesses, with one another, growing in intimacy and vulnerability.

Cultivating intimacy and vulnerability involves walking in transparency and authenticity, allowing others to see our true selves and sharing our deepest thoughts and feelings. "Therefore, having put aside falsehood, each one of you is to speak the truth with his neighbor, for we are members of one another." (Ephesians 4:25 NASB) God calls us to be honest and authentic in our relationships, speaking the truth in love and building trust and intimacy with one another. "Let love be without hypocrisy. Abhor what is evil; cling to what is good. Be devoted to one another in brotherly love; give preference to one another in honor." (Romans 12:9-10 NASB)

Nurturing Trust and Respect

TRUST AND RESPECT ARE the cornerstones of every healthy relationship, and humility plays a vital role in nurturing these qualities. When we humble ourselves before our loved ones, we demonstrate our trust in their judgment and respect for their autonomy. By valuing their perspectives and opinions with humility and grace, we create a foundation of trust and respect that strengthens our bond and withstands the tests of time.

The Bible emphasizes the importance of trust and respect in relationships, highlighting their essential role in fostering unity and harmony. "Let no one deceive you with empty words, for because of these things the wrath of God comes upon the sons of disobedience."(Ephesians 5:6 NASB) God calls us to nurture trust and respect by speaking the truth in love, avoiding deceit and dishonesty that can erode trust and damage relationships. "A friend loves at all times, and a brother is born for adversity." (Proverbs 17:17 NASB) Godly relationships are characterized by love, loyalty, and mutual respect, where trust is built through faithful and consistent actions.

Cultivating trust involves living with integrity and faithfulness, honoring our commitments and demonstrating reliability and consistency in our words and actions. "The one who walks in integrity will experience a blessing, but whoever is perverse in his ways will fall into trouble." (Proverbs 28:6 NASB) God calls us to walk in integrity and faithfulness. Our actions speak louder than words and have the power to build or break trust in relationships. "Let love be without hypocrisy. Abhor what is evil; cling to what is good." (Romans 12:9 NASB) True love is accompanied by genuine respect and honor for one another, valuing each other's worth and treating each other with dignity and consideration.

Practicing Forgiveness and Grace

NO RELATIONSHIP IS perfect, and humility allows us to extend forgiveness and grace when mistakes are made. When we humble ourselves before others, acknowledging our own faults and shortcomings, we cultivate a spirit of humility that makes it easier to forgive those who have wronged us. By offering forgiveness with humility and grace, we release ourselves from bitterness and resentment, paving the way for healing and reconciliation.

Forgiveness stands as a cornerstone of humility, reflecting the divine grace and mercy bestowed upon us by God. The Bible unequivocally underscores the imperative of forgiveness, emphasizing its pivotal role in the Christian life. "And whenever you stand praying, forgive, if you have anything against anyone, so that your Father also who is in heaven may forgive you your trespasses." (Mark 11:25 NASB)

Jesus Himself exhorts His disciples to forgive others, thereby emphasizing the essential nature of forgiveness in the Christian Walk. "For if you forgive others for their transgressions, your heavenly Father will also forgive you." (Matthew 6:14 (NASB) The reciprocal nature of forgiveness underscores its transformative power, both in reconciling relationships and in fostering spiritual growth and renewal.

God calls us to extend forgiveness and grace to one another, reflecting His boundless love and mercy towards us as sinners saved by grace. "And be kind to one another, tender-hearted, forgiving each other, just as God in Christ also has forgiven you."(Colossians 3:13 NASB) Forgiveness is not based on merit but is a gracious gift bestowed upon us by God, and we are called to extend that same grace to others. Practicing forgiveness and grace involves letting go of bitterness, resentment, and anger, and choosing to forgive others as God has forgiven us.

Embracing Growth and Change

HUMILITY OPENS THE door to growth and change in relationships, allowing us to evolve and adapt together over time. When we approach relationships with humility, we recognize that we are not perfect and that there is always room for growth and improvement. By humbly embracing feedback and constructive criticism, we create a culture of growth and learning that strengthens our bond and deepens our connection.

The Bible emphasizes the importance of growth and change in the Christian life, highlighting the transformative power of God's grace and the sanctifying work of the Holy Spirit. "And do not be conformed to this world, but be transformed by the renewing of your mind, so that you may prove what the will of God is, that which is good and acceptable and perfect." (Romans 12:2 NASB) God calls us to embrace growth and change by allowing His Word to renew our minds and transform our hearts, conforming us to the image of Christ. "But grow in the grace and knowledge of our Lord and Savior Jesus Christ. To Him be the glory, both now and to the day of eternity. Amen." (2 Peter 3:18 NASB) God desires for His children to continually grow in grace and knowledge, maturing in their faith and becoming more like Christ with each passing day.

Embracing growth and change involves embracing the process of transformation and renewal, allowing God to work in our lives and relationships for His glory "Therefore if anyone is in Christ, he is a new creature; the old things passed away; behold, new things have come." (2 Corinthians 5:17 NASB) In Christ, we are made new, and old patterns of behavior and thought are replaced by newness of life, enabling us to grow and change according to God's will. "And we all, with unveiled face, beholding the glory of the Lord, are being transformed into the same image from one degree of glory to another. For this comes from the Lord who is the Spirit." (2 Corinthians 3:18 NASB)

Cultivating Gratitude and Appreciation

HUMILITY FOSTERS GRATITUDE and appreciation for the people we love and cherish. When we approach relationships with humility, we recognize the value and importance of our loved ones, expressing gratitude for their presence in our lives. By humbly acknowledging the ways in which others enrich our lives, we deepen our connection and strengthen our bond.

Appreciation is a powerful expression of humility in relationships, reflecting a heart that values and recognizes the worth of others. The Bible emphasizes the importance of appreciating and honoring one another, recognizing the inherent value and worth that each person possesses as a creation of God. "Love one another with brotherly affection. Outdo one another in showing honor." (Romans 12:10 NASB) Paul exhorts believers to love one another with genuine affection and to outdo one another in showing honor, highlighting the importance of appreciating and valuing each other in relationships. "Therefore encourage one another and build one another up, just as you are doing." (1 Thessalonians 5:11 NASB)

The apostle Paul encourages believers to encourage and build one another up, recognizing and affirming the strengths and contributions of each member of the body of Christ.

"And let us consider how to stimulate one another to love and good deeds, not forsaking our own assembling together, as is the habit of some, but encouraging one another; and all the more as you see the day drawing near." (Hebrews 10:24-25 NASB) The writer of Hebrews urges believers to stimulate one another to love and good deeds, emphasizing the importance of encouragement and appreciation in spurring one another on toward spiritual growth and maturity.

Conclusion of Chapter 8

IN THIS CHAPTER, WE have explored the profound impact of humility on nurturing and sustaining healthy, meaningful relationships. Humility fosters empathy, resolves conflicts, deepens intimacy, nurtures trust and respect, promotes forgiveness and grace, embraces growth and change, and cultivates gratitude and appreciation. As we continue to cultivate humility in our relationships, may we strengthen our connections, deepen our bonds, and experience the transformative power of love and understanding.

Chapter 9
The Ultimate Model of Humility

JESUS CHRIST, THE EPITOME of humility, serves as our ultimate model. Journey with us as we explore His life and teachings, drawing inspiration for our own pursuit of humility.

In the vast landscape of human history, there exists one figure whose life serves as the ultimate model of humility—Jesus Christ. In this chapter, we will explore the profound teachings and example of Jesus, examining how his life epitomized humility in its purest form and continues to inspire countless individuals to follow in his footsteps.

The Humble Birth of Jesus

THE STORY OF JESUS begins not in a palace or amidst grandeur, but in humble surroundings—a stable in Bethlehem. Born to a young couple of modest means, Jesus entered the world in humility, wrapped in swaddling clothes and laid in a manger. His birth, announced by angels to lowly shepherds, foreshadowed the humility that would characterize his entire life.

The humble birth of Jesus stands as a profound example of true humility, demonstrating the incomparable love and humility of God incarnate. The birth of Jesus in humble circumstances fulfills the prophecy of the Messiah's humble arrival, as foretold by the prophets of old. "But as for you, Bethlehem Ephrathah, too little to be among the clans of Judah, from you One will go forth for Me to be ruler in Israel. His goings forth are from long ago, from the days of eternity." (Micah 5:2 NASB) The prophet Micah foretells the humble birthplace of the

Messiah in Bethlehem, a small and insignificant town in Judah, highlighting the unexpected nature of His arrival.

The birth of Jesus in a lowly manger in Bethlehem underscores His identification with the poor, marginalized, and humble of society. "And she gave birth to her firstborn son; and she wrapped Him in cloths, and laid Him in a manger, because there was no room for them in the inn." (Luke 2:7 NASB) The Gospel of Luke recounts the humble circumstances surrounding Jesus' birth, as He is laid in a manger due to the lack of space in the inn, reflecting the simplicity and humility of His earthly arrival.

The incarnation of Jesus Christ represents the ultimate act of humility, as the Son of God takes on human flesh and dwells among humanity. The humble birth of Jesus Christ serves as a powerful reminder of God's incomparable love and humility, as He willingly entered into human history to redeem and reconcile humanity to Himself. As we reflect on the humble beginnings of our Savior, may we be inspired to emulate His example of true humility in our lives, serving others with love, compassion, and humility, just as Christ served us.

The Servant King

THROUGHOUT HIS MINISTRY, Jesus embodied the paradoxical nature of humility and greatness. Though he was the Son of God, he willingly took on the role of a servant, washing the feet of his disciples and teaching them that true greatness comes from serving others. He said, "For even the Son of Man did not come to be served, but to serve, and to give His life a ransom for many" (Mark 10:45). Jesus demonstrated that humility is not weakness but strength, not servility but a posture of love and selflessness.

The concept of Jesus as the Servant King epitomizes humility and servant leadership, providing a profound example for all believers to emulate. Jesus' ministry on earth was characterized by servant leadership, as He humbly served others and sacrificially gave of Himself for the sake of humanity. "For even the Son of Man did not come to be served, but to serve, and to give His life a ransom for many." (Mark 10:45 NASB) Jesus Himself declares His mission as one of service, not to be served but to serve others and to give His life as a ransom for many, exemplifying the essence of servant leadership.

One of the most powerful demonstrations of Jesus' servant leadership is seen in His washing of the disciples' feet, a humble act of service and love. "So when He had washed their feet, and taken His garments and reclined at the table again, He said to them, 'Do you know what I have done to you? You call Me Teacher and Lord; and you are right, for so I am. If I then, the Lord and the Teacher, washed your feet, you also ought to wash one another's feet. For I gave you an example that you also should do as I did to you.'" (John 13:12-15 NASB) Jesus' washing of the disciples' feet serves as a powerful illustration of His humility and servant-heartedness, as He teaches His disciples to emulate His example of serving one another with humility and love.

The pinnacle of Jesus' servant leadership is His sacrificial death on the cross, where He willingly laid down His life for the redemption and salvation of humanity. "Greater love has no one than this, that one lay down his life for his friends."(John 15:13 NASB) Jesus' sacrificial death on the cross exemplifies the depths of His love and humility, as He offers Himself as the ultimate sacrifice for the forgiveness of sins, reconciling humanity to God. Jesus' role as the Servant King serves as a powerful model of humble leadership and sacrificial love for all believers to follow.

The Way of the Cross

THE PINNACLE OF JESUS' humility was seen in his journey to the cross. Despite facing betrayal, mockery, and excruciating pain, Jesus humbly submitted to the will of the Father, enduring the ultimate sacrifice for the redemption of humanity. In his final moments on the cross, he prayed, "Father, forgive them, for they know not what they do" (Luke 23:34), exemplifying forgiveness and grace even in the midst of suffering.

Jesus' journey to the cross exemplifies the epitome of humility and sacrificial love, as He willingly embraced suffering and death for the redemption of humanity. "And He was saying to them all, 'If anyone wishes to come after Me, he must deny himself, and take up his cross daily and follow Me.'" (Luke 9:23 NASB) Jesus calls His followers to take up their crosses daily and follow Him, symbolizing a life of self-denial, sacrificial love, and humble obedience to God's will.

The way of the cross is characterized by humility, obedience, and submission to God's will, even in the face of suffering and persecution. "He humbled Himself by becoming obedient to the point of death, even death on a cross." (Philippians 2:8 NASB) The apostle Paul highlights the humility and obedience of Christ in His journey to the cross, as He willingly submitted Himself to the Father's will, even unto death.

Embracing the cross involves surrendering our own desires, ambitions, and comforts for the sake of following Christ and advancing His kingdom. "And He was saying to them all, 'If anyone wishes to come after Me, he must deny himself, and take up his cross daily and follow Me.'"(Luke 9:23 NASB) Jesus' call to take up our crosses daily challenges us to embrace a life of humility, sacrifice, and selflessness, following His example of love and obedience.

Love in Action

JESUS' ENTIRE LIFE was a testament to the power of love in action. He ministered to the poor, healed the sick, and welcomed the outcast with compassion and grace. His teachings challenged societal norms and called for radical love and inclusion. He taught his followers to love their enemies, to forgive those who wronged them, and to show mercy to all. His life exemplified the principle that true humility is rooted in love for God and love for neighbor.

The commandment to love one another lies at the heart of Christian faith and practice, calling believers to demonstrate their love for God by loving others in tangible ways. "A new commandment I give to you, that you love one another, even as I have loved you, that you also love one another. By this all men will know that you are My disciples, if you have love for one another."(John 13:34-35 NASB) Jesus commands His disciples to love one another just as He has loved them, highlighting the transformative power of love in bearing witness to the world. Who are His disciples? We are. The ones who proclaim that we are Christian.

Love in action goes beyond mere words or sentiment, manifesting itself in practical acts of kindness, compassion, and service towards others. "Little children, let us not love with word or with tongue, but in deed and truth." (1

John 3:18 NASB) The apostle John exhorts believers to love not only in word or speech but also in deed and truth, emphasizing the importance of genuine, sacrificial love expressed through tangible actions.

The Resurrection and Exaltation

THE STORY OF JESUS does not end with his death on the cross but culminates in his resurrection and exaltation. Through his resurrection, Jesus conquered sin and death, offering the promise of new life and hope to all who believe in him. He was exalted to the right hand of the Father, where he reigns as Lord and Savior. Yet, even in his exalted state, Jesus remains the ultimate model of humility, forever pointing us to the way of selfless love and service.

The resurrection and exaltation of Jesus Christ mark the culmination of His humble obedience and sacrificial love, demonstrating God's ultimate victory over sin and death. The resurrection of Jesus Christ stands as the ultimate triumph of humility and obedience, as He conquers sin and death through His sacrificial death and victorious resurrection. "He is not here, for He has risen, just as He said. Come, see the place where He was lying." (Matthew 28:6 NASB) The angel's proclamation of Jesus' resurrection confirms the fulfillment of His promise and the victory of life over death, demonstrating God's power and faithfulness.

The exaltation of Jesus Christ to the right hand of God signifies His supreme authority and sovereignty over all creation, as He reigns as Lord and King. "Therefore, God highly exalted Him, and bestowed on Him the name which is above every name, so that at the name of Jesus every knee will bow, of those who are in heaven and on earth and under the earth, and that every tongue will confess that Jesus Christ is Lord, to the glory of God the Father." (Philippians 2:9-11 NASB) Paul declares the exaltation of Jesus Christ to the highest place of honor and authority, acknowledging Him as Lord over all creation and calling believers to worship and confess His lordship.

The resurrection and exaltation of Jesus Christ offer believers the hope of eternal life and exaltation with Him, as they are united with Christ in His death and resurrection. "Blessed be the God and Father of our Lord Jesus Christ, who according to His great mercy has caused us to be born again to a living hope through the resurrection of Jesus Christ from the dead." (1 Peter 1:3 NASB) Peter praises God for His mercy and the living hope that believers have through the resurrection of Jesus Christ, securing their inheritance of eternal life and exaltation in His kingdom.

The resurrection and exaltation of Jesus Christ stand as the pinnacle of God's redemptive plan, demonstrating His victory over sin and death and offering believers the hope of eternal life and exaltation with Christ.

Following the Example of Jesus

AS FOLLOWERS OF JESUS, we are called to emulate his example of humility in our own lives. We are called to humble ourselves before God and before others, to serve with love and compassion, and to live lives marked by forgiveness and grace. Jesus said, "Take my yoke upon you and learn from me, for I am gentle and humble in heart, and you will find rest for your souls" (Matthew 11:29). In following the example of Jesus, we find true rest and fulfillment for our souls.

Jesus' life and teachings provide a model of humility for believers to emulate, calling us to humble ourselves and serve others as He did. "Take My yoke upon you and learn from Me, for I am gentle and humble in heart, and you will find rest for your souls." (Matthew 11:29 NASB) Jesus invites His followers to learn from Him and take on His yoke, which is characterized by gentleness and humility, offering rest for weary souls.

The Transformative Power of Humility

THE LIFE OF JESUS STANDS as a powerful testament to the transformative power of humility. His example has inspired countless individuals throughout history to live lives of selflessness, compassion, and service. By following in his footsteps, we too can experience the profound joy and fulfillment that comes from living a life centered on love and humility.

Humility stands as a beacon of transformation, capable of reshaping hearts, communities, and even nations. Rooted in reverence for God and a genuine regard for others, humility carries the power to heal wounds, mend relationships, and ignite a chain reaction of grace and restoration.

Conclusion of Chapter 9

IN THIS CHAPTER, WE have explored the ultimate model of humility in the life of Jesus Christ. From his humble birth to his sacrificial death and glorious resurrection, Jesus exemplified humility in its purest form. His life serves as an enduring example of love, compassion, and selflessness, inspiring us to follow in his footsteps and live lives marked by humility and grace. As we seek to emulate the example of Jesus, may we find the strength and courage to humble ourselves before God and before others, and to live lives that reflect the transformative power of humility.

Chapter 10
Living a Life of Humility

AS WE CONCLUDE OUR exploration, let's reflect on practical steps to integrate humility into every aspect of our lives, embracing it as a foundational virtue that leads us closer to God and one another.

Humility is not merely a virtue to admire from a distance; it is a way of life to be embraced and lived out daily. In this final chapter, we will explore practical ways to cultivate and embody humility in our everyday lives, recognizing that true humility is not a destination but a journey of continuous growth and transformation.

Embracing Authenticity

LIVING A LIFE OF HUMILITY begins with embracing authenticity—being true to ourselves and others. Authenticity requires us to acknowledge our strengths and weaknesses, to celebrate our successes humbly, and to admit our mistakes with grace. When we embrace authenticity, we create space for genuine connections and meaningful relationships to flourish.

Practicing Gratitude

GRATITUDE IS A CORNERSTONE of humility, reminding us of the blessings we have received and the interconnectedness of all life. By cultivating a spirit of gratitude, we humble ourselves before the generosity of others and recognize the countless gifts and privileges we often take for granted. Practicing gratitude fosters humility by shifting our focus from what we lack to what we have been given.

Cultivating a Learning Mindset

HUMILITY THRIVES IN an environment of curiosity and continuous learning. Embracing a learning mindset means acknowledging that we do not have all the answers and that there is always room for growth and improvement. By humbly seeking knowledge and wisdom from others, we expand our perspectives and deepen our understanding of the world around us.

Serving Others with Compassion

AT THE HEART OF HUMILITY lies a spirit of service and compassion towards others. Humble individuals prioritize the needs of others above their own desires and interests, seeking opportunities to serve and uplift those around them. Whether through acts of kindness, volunteer work, or simply lending a listening ear, living a life of humility means actively seeking ways to make a positive difference in the lives of others.

Embracing Vulnerability

VULNERABILITY IS A hallmark of humility, requiring us to open ourselves up to the possibility of rejection, failure, and disappointment. When we embrace vulnerability with humility, we cultivate deeper connections with others and foster empathy and understanding. By sharing our authentic selves with humility and courage, we create space for intimacy, trust, and authenticity in our relationships.

Practicing Forgiveness

FORGIVENESS IS A POWERFUL expression of humility, releasing us from the burden of resentment and bitterness. When we forgive others with humility and grace, we acknowledge our own imperfections and recognize the humanity in those who have wronged us. By letting go of grudges and extending forgiveness, we free ourselves to experience healing, reconciliation, and inner peace.

Maintaining a Spirit of Humility

LIVING A LIFE OF HUMILITY requires ongoing self-reflection and intentionality. It means resisting the temptation to pride and ego, and instead, choosing the path of humility and grace. By maintaining a spirit of humility in our thoughts, words, and actions, we create a ripple effect of kindness, compassion, and understanding that uplifts and inspires those around us.

Embodying Humility in Leadership

FOR THOSE IN POSITIONS of leadership, humility is especially crucial. True leadership is not about exerting power or control but about serving others with humility and integrity. Humble leaders prioritize the well-being of their team members, listen with empathy and openness, and acknowledge their own limitations. By embodying humility in leadership, they inspire trust, loyalty, and collaboration, fostering a culture of respect and empowerment.

Conclusion of Chapter 10

IN THIS FINAL CHAPTER, we have explored the practical aspects of living a life of humility. From embracing authenticity and practicing gratitude to serving others with compassion and embracing vulnerability, humility manifests itself in myriad ways in our everyday lives. By cultivating a spirit of humility and grace, we create opportunities for growth, connection, and transformation, both within ourselves and in the world around us. As we continue on the journey of living a life of humility, may we be guided by the example of Jesus Christ and inspired by the countless individuals who have humbly walked before us, leaving behind a legacy of love, compassion, and service.

Conclusion:
Embracing the Biblical Path of Humility

AS WE CONCLUDE OUR journey through the profound virtue of humility, we find ourselves standing on holy ground, surrounded by the timeless wisdom and eternal truths of Scripture. Throughout our exploration, we have witnessed the transformative power of humility to shape lives, mend broken relationships, and draw us closer to the heart of God. Now, as we reflect on the lessons learned and the insights gained, let us turn to the Word of God to guide us in our final steps on this sacred journey.

The Biblical Foundation of Humility

FROM GENESIS TO REVELATION, the Bible resounds with the call to humility—a call to walk humbly before our God and with one another. In the book of Proverbs, we are reminded that "Pride goes before destruction, and a haughty spirit before a fall" (Proverbs 16:18). And in the Gospel of Matthew, Jesus declares, "Blessed are the meek, for they shall inherit the earth" (Matthew 5:5). These verses, among countless others, serve as a foundation upon which we build our understanding of humility as a core principle of the Christian life.

The Example of Jesus Christ

AT THE HEART OF OUR journey of humility stands the example of Jesus Christ—the ultimate model of humility and servant leadership. In the Gospel of John, we read of Jesus washing the feet of his disciples, humbly taking on the role of a servant despite being their Lord and Teacher (John 13:1-17). And in the letter to the Philippians, the apostle Paul exhorts believers to "Have this mind among yourselves, which is yours in Christ Jesus, who, though he was in the form of God, did not count equality with God a thing to be grasped, but emptied himself, by taking the form of a servant" (Philippians 2:5-7).

The Call to Humble Ourselves

THROUGHOUT SCRIPTURE, we are repeatedly called to humble ourselves before God and one another. In the book of James, we read, "Humble yourselves before the Lord, and he will exalt you" (James 4:10). And in the first letter of Peter, we are urged, "Clothe yourselves, all of you, with humility toward one another, for 'God opposes the proud but gives grace to the humble'" (1 Peter 5:5).

The Fruit of Humility

THE SCRIPTURES TEACH us that humility bears fruit in our lives and in the world around us. In the book of Micah, we are told, "He has told you, O man, what is good; and what does the Lord require of you but to do justice, and to love kindness, and to walk humbly with your God?" (Micah 6:8). And in the letter to the Galatians, we learn that "the fruit of the Spirit is love, joy, peace, patience, kindness, goodness, faithfulness, gentleness, self-control" (Galatians 5:22-23).

The Promise of Exaltation

FINALLY, SCRIPTURE assures us of the promise of exaltation for those who walk in humility before God. In the Gospel of Luke, Jesus declares, "For everyone who exalts himself will be humbled, and he who humbles himself will be exalted" (Luke 14:11). And in the first letter of James, we are told, "Humble yourselves before the Lord, and he will exalt you" (James 4:10).

Walking Humbly with Our God

AS WE BRING OUR JOURNEY of humility to a close, let us take to heart the timeless truths and eternal promises of Scripture. Let us heed the call to humble ourselves before God and one another, following in the footsteps of our Lord and Savior Jesus Christ. Let us cultivate a spirit of humility in our thoughts, words, and actions, and let us seek to embody the love, compassion, and servant-heartedness of Christ in all that we do.

May we walk humbly with our God, trusting in his grace and leaning on his strength. May we be ever mindful of the example set before us by Jesus Christ, who humbled himself for our sake, and who calls us to do likewise. And may we be empowered by the Holy Spirit to live lives of humility, love, and service, bringing glory to God and blessing to all whom we encounter.

As we journey forward, may the words of Scripture guide us, the example of Jesus inspire us, and the promise of exaltation sustain us. And may we never forget that true greatness is found in humility—a humility that leads to exaltation in the kingdom of God.

Scripture Reading Plan

This 12-week reading plan is designed to complement each chapter of this book, providing a biblical foundation and spiritual nourishment for the journey of humility.

Week 1: Understanding Humility

- Day 1: Psalm 139:23-24
- Day 2: Proverbs 3:5-6
- Day 3: Philippians 2:3-4
- Day 4: Micah 6:8
- Day 5: Luke 14:11
- Day 6: Romans 12:3
- Day 7: Matthew 11:29-30

Week 2: Examples of Humility in the Bible

- Day 1: Genesis 12:1-4
- Day 2: Exodus 3:1-15
- Day 3: Luke 1:26-38
- Day 4: John 13:1-17
- Day 5: Philippians 2:5-11
- Day 6: 1 Peter 5:5-7
- Day 7: Hebrews 12:1-3

WEEK 3: THE NATURE of True Humility

- Day 1: Psalm 25:9
- Day 2: Proverbs 11:2
- Day 3: Isaiah 66:2
- Day 4: Matthew 5:5
- Day 5: Romans 12:16
- Day 6: 1 Corinthians 13:4-7
- Day 7: James 4:10

Week 4: Humility in Action

- Day 1: Psalm 37:3-4
- Day 2: Isaiah 58:10-11
- Day 3: Matthew 23:11-12
- Day 4: Romans 12:10-13
- Day 5: Galatians 5:13
- Day 6: Ephesians 4:1-3
- Day 7: Philippians 2:3-8

Week 5: The Rewards of Humility

- Day 1: Psalm 84:10-12
- Day 2: Proverbs 22:4
- Day 3: Matthew 23:12
- Day 4: James 4:6
- Day 5: 1 Peter 5:5-6
- Day 6: Philippians 4:6-7
- Day 7: Colossians 3:12

Week 6: Overcoming Pride

- Day 1: Psalm 51:17
- Day 2: Proverbs 16:18
- Day 3: Isaiah 2:11

- Day 4: Luke 18:9-14
- Day 5: Romans 12:3
- Day 6: 2 Corinthians 12:9-10
- Day 7: James 4:10

Week 7: Cultivating Humility in Daily Life

- Day 1: Psalm 131
- Day 2: Proverbs 3:34
- Day 3: Matthew 6:1-4
- Day 4: Luke 6:27-36
- Day 5: Philippians 2:14-16
- Day 6: Colossians 3:12-14
- Day 7: 1 Peter 3:8-9

Week 8: Humility and Leadership

- Day 1: Psalm 78:70-72
- Day 2: Proverbs 11:2
- Day 3: Matthew 20:25-28
- Day 4: Mark 10:42-45
- Day 5: Luke 22:24-27
- Day 6: 1 Timothy 3:1-7
- Day 7: Titus 1:7-9

Week 9: The Power of Humble Service

- Day 1: Psalm 100
- Day 2: Proverbs 19:17
- Day 3: Matthew 25:34-40
- Day 4: Mark 9:35
- Day 5: Luke 10:25-37
- Day 6: Acts 20:35
- Day 7: Romans 12:6-8

Week 10: Humility in Relationships

- Day 1: Psalm 133
- Day 2: Proverbs 15:33
- Day 3: Matthew 5:23-24
- Day 4: Romans 15:1-2
- Day 5: 1 Corinthians 13:4-7
- Day 6: Ephesians 4:1-3
- Day 7: Philippians 2:1-4

Week 11: The Ultimate Model of Humility

- Day 1: Isaiah 53:1-12

- Day 2: Matthew 11:29
- Day 3: John 13:1-17
- Day 4: Philippians 2:5-11
- Day 5: Colossians 1:15-20
- Day 6: Hebrews 12:1-3
- Day 7: 1 Peter 2:21-24

Week 12: Living a Life of Humility

- Day 1: Psalm 37:7-9
- Day 2: Proverbs 22:4
- Day 3: Matthew 23:11-12
- Day 4: Romans 12:1-2
- Day 5: Galatians 5:22-26
- Day 6: Ephesians 4:1-3
- Day 7: Philippians 4:4-9